INDIA'S HEROES

A TRIBUTE

ADITYA KASHYAP

Dedication

This book is dedicated to all the soldiers of the Indian Armed Forces

FOREWORD

The Army, Navy and Air Force of India have always stood as cultural and civilizational icons for the people of this Nation. They have served to define the inner-most spirit of the people of this sub- continent. The two greatest epics of the country – The Ramayana and the Mahabharata are not so much about war but about warriors.

Nothing brings out the ethos of India more than the composition of its leadership in the 1971 war, where its Armed Forces helped in the creation of a new nation – Bangladesh. A Kashmiri Brahmin Prime Minister, a Sikh Foreign Minister, a Defence Minister from one of its historically excluded castes and communities, a Parsi Army Chief, A Sikh Theatre Commander with a Jewish Officer for his Chief of Staff–led the Indian Army, Navy and Air Force.

Upholding the values of valour and selfless sacrifice have always been the spontaneous urging of India and its people. Nowhere have these characteristics stood out more than the celebration by India of the gallantry with which our young officers and soldiers acquitted themselves in the Kargil and the Galwan conflicts and gave their lives for the country. The responses of our adversaries, on the other hand, were characterized by denial and obfuscation, bordering on shame.

It is heartening, therefore, to see the publication of the book 'India's Heroes-A Tribute' by Aditya Kashyap. The book represents the inner voice of a 12-year-old, 7th grader, who brings out in proud detail the valour and spirit of nationhood displayed by 21 recipients of the highest military decoration, bestowed by India upon its sons and daughters who have displayed distinguished acts of valour during wartime.

Param Vir Chakra translates as the "Wheel of the Ultimate Brave". His poems on these warriors are in the finest tradition of the Veer Gatha– the song of the Faithful – the genre of Indian Art and Literature that have celebrated its warriors from times immemorial.

It has been a privilege for me to acknowledge through this foreword, the deep expression of national pride that Aditya is bound to stir among his peer group in the country and the diaspora abroad.

I would like to wish Aditya Kashyap more power to his pen. May he and his generation of boys and girls serve the nation in the finest traditions laid down in his writings.

Vice Admiral Ganesh Mahadevan (Retd),
Indian Navy
Bangalore, August 2022

PARAM VIR CHAKRA

The Param Vir Chakra is India's highest award for gallantry during wartime, awarded for the most conspicuous acts of bravery or some daring or pre-eminent act of valour or self-sacrifice, in the presence of the enemy, whether on land, at sea, or in the air. The decoration may be awarded posthumously or in person.

CONTENTS

Preface 9

Acknowledgements 11

My Salute To The Indian Armed Forces 13

1. Major Somnath Sharma 14

2. Lance Naik
    (later Honorary Captain)
    Karam Singh 16

3. 2ⁿᵈ Lieutenant (Later Major) Rama Raghoba Rane 18

4. Naik Jadunath Singh 20

5. Company Havildar Major Piru Singh Shekhawat 22

6. Captain Gurbachan Singh Salaria 24

7. Major (later Lieutenant Colonel) Dhan Singh Thapa 26

8. Subedar Joginder Singh 28

9. Major Shaitan Singh 30

10. Company Quarter Master Havildar Abdul Hamid 32

11. Lieutenant Colonel Ardeshir Burzorji Tarapore 34

12. Lance Naik Albert Ekka 36

13. Flying Officer
    Nirmal Jit Singh Sekhon 38

14. 2ⁿᵈ Lieutenant Arun Khetarpal 40

15. Major (later Colonel)
    Hoshiar Singh 42

16. Naib Subedar (later Subedar Major and Honorary Captain)
    Bana Singh 44

17. Major Ramaswamy Parameswaran 46

18. Captain Manoj Kumar Pandey 48

19. Grenadier (Later Subedar Major and Honorary Captain)
    Yogendra Singh Yadav 50

20. Rifleman (Later Subedar Major) Sanjay Kumar 52

21. Captain Vikram Batra 54

Gallery 57

PREFACE

India's Heroes - A Tribute, is a short book that was written for the sole purpose of honouring our valiant soldiers and officers who went beyond the call of duty and made the ultimate sacrifice to ensure that our beloved country remains free from foreign intrusion. This is a book of twenty-one poems, one for each awardee of the Param Vir Chakra, that describes in detail the sharp, split-second decisions that they made, while keeping their fighting spirit to ensure the safety of our motherland.

I bow my head in reverence towards every solider of the Armed Forces and these 21 indomitable men and their families, who displayed extraordinary grit in the face of great adversity.

It is my sincere hope and belief that this book will reach the hands of every proud Indian and they will join me in paying rich tribute to the sacrifices of these men.

I have read various books and researched on the internet to collect the details for this book. I seek the readers' indulgence for any inadequacies.

ACKNOWLEDGEMENTS

My heartfelt prayers and gratitude to God, my parents, and my grandparents, now and always.

I thank all my family and teachers for supporting me along this journey.

I am indebted to Vice Admiral Ganesh Mahadevan (Retd.) for his articulate words of encouragement and bringing out the essence of my book in his Foreword.

I enjoyed many conversations with servicemen and ex-servicemen of the Indian Army, Navy, and Air Force. I sincerely thank Captain (IN) Rajagopal Reddy BN (Retd.) and Flt Lt Partha Datta (Retd.). Thank You Sirs, for sparing your precious time. Your stories will stay with me forever.

MY SALUTE TO THE INDIAN ARMED FORCES

Army, Air Force, Navy. All rolled into one,
a formidable combination that will put you on the run.
We go about our work, without fear every day,
because we know they stand guard and will put the enemy to sway.

Words cannot describe the reverence they deserve,
so I pen a poem and that reverence I preserve.
A noble profession, to serve the country,
India's well protected with a million-strong army.

A tribute to the soldiers who laid down their lives,
may they Rest in Eternal Peace, with closed eyes.
Major Somnath and Captain Batra, just to name a few,
their sacrifice will be remembered like sweet honey dew.

My last few words, to convey my thanks,
to our courageous protectors, in olive green pants.
On every single day, we remember you,
and say a silent 'thanks' for all that you do!

MAJOR SOMNATH SHARMA

Year of Award: 1947
Regiment: 4th Battalion, Kumaon Regiment

Major Somnath Sharma

A passionate leader from the time he was born,
joined the Indian Army, to protect the country he was sworn.
He passed out of I.M.A in the year of 1942,
he was then a commissioned officer with the test that he's through.

He had a fractured arm but was deployed with his troops,
to stop this officer, it would take nukes.
He was the gallant commander of the Kumaon Battalion,
and he charged to the front like an inspired stallion.

He was to stop an attack, threatening our might,
and what followed at the scene, was his inspiring last fight.
Picking up a machine gun, he destroyed the enemy,
when an enemy shell exploded! What treachery!

When the smoke cleared, Major Somnath lay among the dead,
shooting down the enemy, his soldiers rushed ahead.
He inspired his men even with his last breath,
his gallantry earned him a laurel wreath.

The gallant commander of 4 Kumaon,
he fought the odds and held his ground.
He was awarded the Param Vir Chakra, for his noble role,
in securing our position, and on Kashmir, getting a hold.

LANCE NAIK
(LATER HONORARY CAPTAIN)
KARAM SINGH

Year of Award: 1948
Regiment: 1st Battalion, Sikh Regiment

Lance Naik Karam Singh

He fought at a time when the future was unclear,
he never knew what would happen to his peers.
But he fought on with a steady mind,
clearing bunker after bunker, he kept on the grind.

Lance Naik Karam Singh excelled in his work,
but one day during a war a stray bullet lurked.
It caught him on his arm, but he continued to fight,
with all his mustered strength he shone a beam of light.

Despite his serious injuries he set his priorities main,
and proceeded to save the lives of countless soldiers in pain.
He cleared the road and created a steady path,
for other valiant Indian Forces to showcase their wrath.

Karam Singh proved his worth on the battlefield that day,
with his valiant efforts and skilled shooting, he held the enemy at bay.
The name of his, will be forever etched, in the history books to come,
with a Param Vir Chakra he retired, he deserves a beat of the drum.

2ND LIEUTENANT (LATER MAJOR) RAMA RAGHOBA RANE

Year of Award: 1948
Regiment: Bombay Sappers Regiment, Corps of Engineers

Second Lieutenant Rama Raghoba Rane

Second Lieutenant Rane, was one of those, with an absolutely brilliant mind,
he displayed exemplary knowledge and solutions, he could find.
He joined the Engineering Corps of the Indian Army one day,
and was immediately under the influence of fellow great minds on display.

And how great he was, that he shot up the ranks with speed,
being commissioned into the Bombay Sappers, his intellect was of need.
One day, the country was at war, and he was commissioned on the front line,
with an armored battalion of tanks, they had to be careful of stealthy mines.

Up ahead the long road, was a mighty blockade to stop the advance,
of the rumbling Indian machinery, with their formidable and intimidating stance.
The Indian Army worked day and night, without any food or rest,
working hard to remove the blockade, and proceed with their ultimate test.

A new and formidable challenge arose, after the blockade was finally clear,
the mines of the enemy army were scattered, and with machinery they
would interfere.
2nd Lieutenant Rane's plan was courageous, daring and bold,
but was a plan that would risk lives and could slip out of Indian control.

The officer went on to crawl in front of the tanks, neutralizing every shell,
so that the path for Indian success was clear, their advance was in propel.
He painlessly went ahead with the task and made sure no mine was left unturned,
if not for his valiant actions of strength, our Indian tanks would have simply burned.

For his strategy, thinking and valiant efforts, he was awarded the PVC,
his memory shall live on, for years to come, nobody can disagree.
And for this honoured officer, that once stood strong, his actions shall live on in time,
his noble role played a vital part in keeping our tanks prime.

NAIK JADUNATH SINGH

Year of Award: 1948
Regiment: 1st Battalion, Rajput Regiment

Naik Jadunath Singh

The plucky young man was faced with a dream,
to become a mighty wrestler, for him would have been the cream.
But his parents were not for it, they felt it was a waste of hope,
but that did not stop him, as he climbed his mental slope.

When he joined the Indian Army, it seemed like the path to take,
but he joined at a time, when India was in British remake.
He sat away from others, observing his vegetarian rule,
but when a British officer challenged him, he would not be taken for a fool.

A day after the incident, he got into his wrestling wear,
and single-handedly knocked down, two men without a care.
Everything was well, until one day, India was in battle,
Naik Jadunath, with his platoon, was on orders to kill and tackle.

But his platoon was a small one, consisting of only nine men,
facing the enemy outnumbered, his platoon constructed a den.
But he had a plan, and what a great plan it was,
daring and bold as he is, lives could be lost in mass.

His men placed themselves apart and fired from different flanks,
tricking the enemy into thinking, that India had brought out tanks!
It was soon hard to manage, and all his men lay on the ground,
breathing with little hope, when Naik Jadunath did something profound.

Injured as he was, he started firing his gun with fury,
inspiring his men to no bounds, enemy blood spilled, it was gory.
But after a valiant effort, his nine men lay on the ground, now dead,
and what followed was a scene that the enemy would dread.

In a relentless show of valour, he drew up his knife to fight,
and broke the backs of the enemy, displaying his military might.
But all it took was two shots. BANG! and the valiant hero lay dead,
India shall eternally mourn his sacrifice and his bloodshed.

Naik Jadunath was awarded the Param Vir Chakra, for his gallant actions in war,
his death was not in vain, we gained back what was ours!

COMPANY HAVILDAR MAJOR PIRU SINGH SHEKHAWAT

Year of Award: 1948
Regiment: 6th Battalion, Rajputana Rifles

Company Havildar Major Piru Singh Shekhawat

Indian forces crept in the dead darkness of the night,
they had the element of surprise, now they had to put up a fight.
It would not be easy, as they were outnumbered,
their only saving grace was that the enemy would be in a slumber.

As they reached the dead zone, the sun was in rise,
now was the time for them to open their eyes.
One false step could jeopardize the safety,
of every Indian solider within meters of eighty.

Mines had been laid, but none were lighted,
but soon after, the Indian troops were sighted.
Grenades were launched and forty men were killed,
within less than half an hour, the Indian side was grilled.

But one man, Piru Shekhawat, stood strong on the Indian side,
charging towards bunkers, some leverage he was to provide.
The enemy was helpless in front of his commanding charge,
many an enemy soldier fell dead because of his barge.

And then, as he headed towards a bunker, a bullet struck his neck,
he did not take any notice, not even bothering to check.
He moved ahead with strength, when he suddenly collapsed,
of pain and fatigue, time suddenly lapsed.

But what followed next was a relentless show of might,
he found some grenades next to him and gathered his remaining fight.
He destroyed the last two bunkers, when a grenade was hurled at him,
when he thought "It's all over", but a miracle was suddenly dim.

The grenade did not explode, and he seized the opportunity,
giving it back to its owners, it decimated the last two enemies.
But Piru had breathed his last, his gallantry shall be remembered,
for his valiant fighting spirit so strong, the enemy was dismembered.

CAPTAIN GURBACHAN SINGH SALARIA

Year of Award: 1961
Regiment: 3rd Battalion, 1 Gorkha Regiment

Captain Gurbachan Singh Salaria

He was sent on a peace mission, one that was not facile,
a volatile environment faced his troops, in the Congo and in the Nile.
Many rebel groups had joined forces, and were working hand in hand,
and how strong they were, that they fell upon two soldiers who were trying to
meet their demands.

Captain Salaria was a man of truth and strength, and those qualities he put
to good use,
when he was summoned by his superior, he introduced himself, with a quick
and brief salute.
His mind worked rapidly and soon he knew exactly what he was to do,
with armoured carriers at his disposal, he started moving with two.

With his small force of only nineteen men, they reached the battlefield,
they were heavily outnumbered, but his valiant nature refused to let him yield.
With a mighty roar of "Give no quarter", he fell upon them in fight,
destroying every one, he showcased his military might.

As he started clearing the enemy, an ambush from behind a wall,
hit the brave Captain on his back, but it did not make him look small.
Taking no notice of his painful injury, he fought ahead with grit,
when there was no enemy left, his men gave a cheer but Captain Salaria had
taken a hit.

Only then did his men notice his pain, and rushed him back to home base,
the valiant commander died a hero, staring adversity in the face.
His bravery and sacrifice shall definitely be remembered, for many millennia
to come,
the valiant Captain ascended into the stars, a legend he had become.

MAJOR (LATER LIEUTENANT COLONEL) DHAN SINGH THAPA

Year of Award: 1962
Regiment: 1st Battalion, 8 Gorkha Regiment

Major Dhan Singh Thapa

He was part of the fiercest regiment, one that was made to kill,
he was a proud solider of the Gorkhas, his enemies had a chill.
Major Dhan Singh Thapa was a man, who would not stop till the end,
he instilled his valiant qualities and had an influence on his men.

It was a gloomy day for India, when a mighty foe attacked,
the Army was deployed on orders to keep India fully intact.
And with this order came, the deadliest regiment of all,
the Gorkha Regiment was on standby and was ready to make them fall.

On one day it happened so, that Major Thapa was sent into battle,
even with a small force of his soldiers, the enemy was rattled.
His spirit was admired, and his energy was like a fully charged battery,
but one quality of him, was his precise and accurate strategy.

During a battle of raw strength, his platoon faced a problem,
the enemy brought out tanks, which marched in single column.
His base was soon captured but Major Thapa could not bear,
to see his post and his men fall, he attacked without a care.

At the end of the perilous battle, the saddening news came in,
Major Thapa and his soldiers had perished. How sad were their kin.
But by miracle of all miracles, a few months passed,
when Major Thapa returned home. With joy, India was flabbergast!

It turned out that after all, Major Thapa was taken captive,
when he returned to home base, he was the same man, fit and active.
Retiring as a Lieutenant Colonel, he earned the highest award,
for his gallantry and actions, when he was abroad.

SUBEDAR JOGINDER SINGH

Year of Award: 1962

Regiment: 1st Battalion, Sikh Regiment

Subedar Joginder Singh

His retirement was in sight, when the country was in fight,
his commander gave him an assignment, to stop the advancing might.
A formidable enemy faced them, with weapons more advanced,
that could defeat us within days, without even a glance.

Subedar Singh moved ahead, and used his experience to their benefit,
analyzing the battlefield, complete with boulders it was fit.
And these boulders, in the battle, would provide them with natural cover,
from the enemy's raining bullets, as they would soon discover.

And soon the battle commenced, with firing and heat,
the enemy was given a befitting thrashing as a treat.
But they soon returned in numbers, and launched a fierce attack,
that martyred many of our soldiers and sent them home in a sack.

This infuriated Subedar Singh, and he started fighting fierce with a roar,
decimating the strong enemy, he charged ahead on score.
But he soon ran out of ammunition, and they started to fall apart,
with their remaining strength they mustered, they ran ahead with heart.

The valiant soldier was soon taken captive, and died as a prisoner in jail,
his gallantry shall be remembered, for his strength and utmost detail.
He was awarded the Param Vir Chakra in braving his last fight,
and giving a befitting reply to the enemy through his relentless military might.

MAJOR SHAITAN SINGH

Year of Award: 1962
Regiment: 13th Battalion, Kumaon Regiment

Major Shaitan Singh

He earned and commanded respect from one and all,
from his seniors to his men, his reputation he installed.
He wanted to prove his determination, and prove it he would do,
his raw courage was loved, such people are only few.

He valiantly fought on although he knew his chances were bleak,
his fighting spirit in combat, made two thousand soldiers look weak.
A mighty army faced him, but the officer stood his ground,
motivating soldiers from trench to trench, a bullet strayed around.

It caught him on his arm and his men requested him to retire,
but he truly led from the front, continuing to inspire.
In the Battle of Rezang La, many Indians bid farewell,
but for every single Indian life, seven enemy soldiers fell.

Under his steady and able guidance, the Indian Army pushed through,
Rezang La was overrun, but Major Shaitan never withdrew.
Every Indian soldier died facing the enemy, weapon in hand,
his sacrifice shall be remembered, as well as his command.

COMPANY QUARTER MASTER HAVILDAR ABDUL HAMID

Year of Award: 1965
Regiment: 4th Battalion, The Grenadiers

Company Quarter Master Havildar Abdul Hamid

The strong, young man was an ace in sports, swimming, wrestling, the lot,
he wanted to continue his wrestling dream, but his parents were not to be bought.
Their dream of him was to settle down and start a life of spirit,
but the ambitious young man was adamant for one, that was full of zeal with no limit.

He decided to join the Indian Army, and the gruesome training for him was fun,
a crack shot he was and his progress helped him, to beat them all in the long run.
During his stint of training for the Indian Army, the country went to fight,
and after a few years of gaining experience, he showcased his military might.

He set out on orders, to command the armoured jeeps,
which was essential for a needed win, our freedom is ours to keep.
And when his men were in the thick of battle, the camouflage was perfect,
that not even a single tank of the Indian Army was hit to any effect.

When Abdul Hamid turned his gun to hit the first enemy tank,
his driver was hit and slumped forward, as was his jeep on the flank.
In a show of camaraderie, Abdul Hamid lifted his injured driver on his strong shoulder,
and wasting no time, evacuated him, to a safe and secure boulder.

After this episode, Abdul was alone, with no one else to support his gun,
but the valiant solider was undeterred, shooting down seven tanks on the run.
But by the time he got to the eighth tank, the enemy was determined to stop him,
they fired a few shots directly on his vehicle, which his helmet also skimmed.

Abdul Hamid's second shot took down the eighth tank,
but the ninth and final tank alive, shot down his jeep on the banks.
The gallant soldier died on the spot, his clothes covered in blood,
he fell down, dead, as his body sank right into the mud.

Abdul Hamid shall be remembered for his valiant efforts in combat,
for effectively bombing the enemy threats, that existed in forms of tanks.
He was awarded the Param Vir Chakra for his gallant and noble role,
in safeguarding India's freedom and keeping it fully whole.

LIEUTENANT COLONEL ARDESHIR BURZORJI TARAPORE

Year of Award: 1965
Regiment: 17th Battalion, Poona Horse Regiment

Lieutenant Colonel Ardeshir Burzorji Tarapore

In Pre-Independent India, a force of soldiers was formed,
they were called the Hyderabad Lancers, and they were fully prepared to storm.
But when Hyderabad became part of India, the lancers had to dissolve,
and this order meant, that their soldiers had to dis-involve.

When General El Edroos surrendered to General Chaudhary of the Indian Military,
a particular officer was also transferred, in a system like a tributary.
And this officer's name was Lt. Col Tarapore, he was instantly loved by all,
for his kind and gentle nature, and his strength which was quite a haul.

In a matter of a few weeks time, India was engaged in battle,
the Army's 17 Poona Horse was sent, out with their tanks they rattled.
And the Commanding Officer of Poona Horse was an able man,
it was Lt. Col Tarapore! And he was armed with a plan.

During the battle of tanks, the Indian Army got the upper hand,
with his men destroying numerous tanks, under their officer's stable command.
But his hand had taken a graze, from a stray bullet in the field,
despite his visible injury, the officer would not yield.

He turned back to face the enemy, in his trusty Tank of Might,
and from then on was a show of relentless military fight.
The enemy took a pounding and learnt a lesson that day,
the Indian Army was on guard, and would never let India astray.

But in that very battle, the enemy tanks regrouped,
and with their remaining numbers, they formed a big troop.
But despite this intimidating sight, the officer and his men stood strong,
fighting for every inch of land, they managed to move ahead long.

At the end, there were just a few tanks, a few on either side,
when Colonel Tarapore moved into the clearing, his tank was hit on guide.
The gallant officer passed away, but his death was not in vain,
for India won that battle, and our freedom was maintained.

LANCE NAIK ALBERT EKKA

Year of Award: 1971
Regiment: 14th Battalion, The Brigade of the Guards

Lance Naik Albert Ekka

Eager to join the Indian Army, he enrolled on his birthday,
always wanting to get deployed, he got his chance in a sway.
Tasked with liberating a sector with his team, they swiftly moved ahead,
when a barrage of gunfire brought them down and many fell dead.

Many soldiers had already fallen and he himself took a hit,
he charged up the stairs and dashed up a wall. He would never quit.
The enemy didn't sight him as he crawled towards them,
with a swift move he silenced the gun and staggered out to his men.

Fighting for his life in his battered, bleeding body, he tried to move ahead,
but his injuries took a toll on him as he fell dead.
Pivotal he was in the success of the operation but paid for it with his life,
he was awarded the Param Vir Chakra and wore death like a badge of pride.

FLYING OFFICER
NIRMAL JIT SINGH SEKHON

Year of Award: 1971
Regiment: No. 18 Squadron, Indian Air Force

Flying Officer Nirmal Jit Singh Sekhon

Very few truly know about this mysterious battle in the sky,
two heroes fought valiantly, to secure our territory up high.
A swarm of enemy pilots threatened the security of our land,
the Air Force was on alert, radars were always scanned.

But one particular pilot, soared high up in the air,
dodging enemy bullets, his aircraft began to tear.
His name was Nirmal Jit Sekhon, and he faced something rare,
contact with base was lost, and six aircraft chased him in the air.

A dogfight ensued, and one that was a sight to see,
only one Indian jet soared, although there were in the enemy: three.
Slowly by slowly, inch by inch, Sekhon lost control,
bullets shred through his gnat, the flight system saw a hole.

Seeing no way to recover his aircraft, Sekhon had only one choice,
pulling the ejector handle, he shot out. Rejoice!
But all was not safe as the ground was a few meters away,
his parachute failed to open, he is missing to this day.

This valiant officer shall be remembered, for putting away to flight,
six lethal aircraft that would have threatened India's might.
He was awarded the Param Vir Chakra for his brave and noble role,
in securing India's safety, and preventing, in our freedom, a hole.

2ND LIEUTENANT ARUN KHETARPAL

Year of Award: 1971
Regiment: 17th Battalion, Poona Horse Regiment

2nd *Lieutenant Arun Khetarpal*

He looked every inch like an officer, so it was the path he was meant to take,
when he joined the Indian Army and departed in its wake.
Gallant commander of the Famagusta, he didn't withdraw an inch,
even when he received orders, he never flinched.

He destroyed seven enemy tanks that were retreating in speed,
only one was left standing when he tried to intercede.
Both fired at the same time but his cannon missed it's mark,
when the enemy shell hit him, he died, igniting a spark.

The Param Vir Chakra he received, for his gallantry and service,
he went beyond the call of duty. Tanks, he'd never miss.
The youngest officer ever to have received such an award,
he had made his mark, and the parents were proud of their ward.

MAJOR (LATER COLONEL) HOSHIAR SINGH

Year of Award: 1971
Regiment: 3rd Battalion, The Grenadiers

Major Hoshiar Singh

From the time he was born, he had but one dream,
to serve the Indian Army with passion and gleam.
The Indian Army was the only thing that he ever spoke about.
so when he joined his job of passion, it seemed expectable throughout.

It was a few months past his milestone, when India went to war,
against a formidable enemy that could cripple our military power.
Major Hoshiar was put in command of the Army's 3rd Grenadier battalion,
they charged out with weapons, looking like black stallions.

As they reached the battlefield, it seemed like a barren land,
when the relentless firing started, Major Hoshiar took command.
They were heavily outnumbered and were under intense enemy shells,
undeterred, he led the charge and got the enemy on the run to hell.

However, the enemy reacted and put in several counter attacks,
one that disabled the MMG, this had many impacts.
The strategic officer had realized it's profound need,
and running towards the gun, started firing it in speed.

This valiant action of Major Singh was one that saved the day,
the Indian Army had the upper hand, the enemy was now prey.
Major Hoshiar Singh went from trench to trench, encouraging his men,
till the enemy had retreated, his guard was never down and we eventually
won once again.

Major Hoshiar Singh was awarded the Param Vir Chakra for his valiant
actions in war,
for his dauntless leadership and fighting spirit, his injury he ignored.
This poem is but an ode to a solider who grappled with fight.
his bravery and honour shall be remembered for showcasing his military might.

NAIB SUBEDAR (LATER SUBEDAR MAJOR AND HONORARY CAPTAIN) BANA SINGH

Year of Award: 1987

Regiment: 8th Battalion, Jammu and Kashmir Light Infantry (8 JAK LI)

Naib Subedar Bana Singh

He led the climb to the Quaid top and captured it in the process,
with a task force of only five men, the enemy was whom he suppressed.
A fitting tribute to the brave soldier was renaming the post 'Bana Top',
now, the Indian Army mans the post, reaping a good crop.

While guns were used in the battle, it was the thinking that saved the day,
the enemy was safely in a bunker while the Indians were astray.
Keeping his wits, he ducked low and stopped the cover fire,
to investigate, the enemy came out and went back in a pyre.

With a smile of victory on their faces, the soldiers moved back,
not a single man took a hit as they walked back on the track.
Every soldier was awarded medals for their courage and bravery,
while their commander was awarded the Param Vir Chakra for his
noble gallantry.

MAJOR RAMASWAMY PARAMESWARAN

Year of Award: 1987
Regiment: 8th Battalion, Mahar Regiment attached to
Indian Peace-keeping Force

Major Ramaswamy Parameswaran

A major crisis was brewing, one that would threaten India itself,
the Lankan Tigers wanted a separate state as a record in the shelf.
The Indian Army was asked to mediate, and the regiment responsible stepped forward,
the Mahar Regiment was on alert, and Major Parameswaran gave the orders.

When the Indian Army landed in Lanka, the situation looked grim,
refugee camps had been set up, it looked worse than a film.
Major Parameswaran was commander and started moving with speed,
intelligence was confirmed, they had to proceed.

But despite his busy schedule, the officer always found time,
to visit the refugee camps, and ring a bell of chime.
Children loved this tall solider, who always brought them sweets,
his kindness shall be remembered, and it shall never cease.

When his platoon was returning to base, they were ambushed on attack,
by a better-equipped militant force, they valiantly fought back.
They retired to a safe cover, and made a retaliation scheme,
when the militants were in sight, his men launched an attack, supreme.

And how fierce that attack was, that the enemy group broke up,
it seemed that we won the day, when they returned from behind a shrub.
Despite the unawareness, the officer valiantly charged on,
as he stepped into the clearing, a bullet hit him on his palm.

His men asked him to evacuate, but the officer refused,
charging towards the militants, his injury was but a bruise.
But alas! Despite his bravery, a bullet struck with a thud,
the fearless solider on his chest, he fell down in blood.

His death charged up his men, and they launched an attack so strong,
that the once stronger enemy, to escape, ran long.
What an impact his death had, that even his watch had stopped,
the brave and valiant officer was the pride of the army's crop.

This poem is but an ode, to a solider who laid down his life,
in the face of great adversity, he displayed relentless fight.
Major Parameswaran was awarded the Param Vir Chakra, his death was not in vain,
I bow my head in reverence, to the officer who disregarded his pain.

CAPTAIN MANOJ KUMAR PANDEY

Year of Award: 1999
Regiment: 1st Battalion, 11 Gorkha Regiment

Captain Manoj Kumar Pandey

He faced a difficult childhood, but he didn't utter a scream,
he always chased his passion, and eventually earned esteem.
The death of his commanding officer spurred him ahead,
faced two hostiles and got them on the run instead.

Commissioned into the Gorkha Rifles, he always led from the front,
took an audacious decision and bore even the brunt.
He joined the Army for a reason, and what a reason it was!
to win the Param Vir Chakra! He is now among the stars.

A mandatory stay on the peaks was coming to an end,
when the brave, young officer volunteered to stay ahead.
Playing with local kids was something he enjoyed,
a gentle horse he was, but could turn ruthless when deployed.

He himself led the climb with his outnumbered men,
the odds were stacked against him, the enemy even had a den.
Keeping these thoughts in mind, he bravely marched ahead,
to be greeted by enemy fire, many soldiers fell dead.

Clearing bunkers one after one with a lion-like roar,
as he rushed to the fourth bunker, a volley of bullets soared.
Bullet wounds all over his body, he rushed ahead with mettle,
when an MMG suddenly fired, and hit him on his temple!

Mad with grief and anger at seeing their comrade down,
the Indian Soldiers went on a rampage and brought the enemy to the ground.
His bravery shall be remembered for centuries to come,
he won the Param Vir Chakra, but in the process, succumbed.

GRENADIER (LATER SUBEDAR MAJOR AND HONORARY CAPTAIN) YOGENDRA SINGH YADAV

Year of Award: 1999
Regiment: 18th Battalion, The Grenadiers

Grenadier Yogendra Singh Yadav

Not many people have the courage to make a difficult choice,
but this courageous man went ahead with poise.
He volunteered to return to his comrades and his base,
when the country was fighting at a crucial state.

Grenadier Yogendra Singh Yadav was a man of strength,
his hard work paid off in full length.
At that point he became one of India's most lethal,
a Ghatak he was, one who was integral.

On one dark night they moved in stealthy treads,
separated from his crew he crept ahead.
With seven commandos in hand, he launched a plan,
just before execution, the shooting began.

The enemy fired relentlessly, till they reached his crew,
they had breathed their last, all but a few.
A coin in his pocket was his unlikely savior,
and gave the valiant soldier another chance in favor.

With his battered body, he stealthily moved ahead,
and caught up with the enemy shooting them dead.
A warning he gave to his beloved Indian side,
who repelled the attack, in that same stride.

Grenadier Yogendra Singh Yadav retired with merit,
if there is one thing to learn: It is to fully commit.
He earned India's highest medal for gallantry and bravery,
the Param Vir Chakra for braving his serious injury.

RIFLEMAN (LATER SUBEDAR MAJOR) SANJAY KUMAR

Year of Award: 1999
Regiment: 13th Battalion, J & K Rifles (JAK RIF)

Rifleman Sanjay Kumar

At his long-awaited time of marriage, a telegram was sent,
a direct order it was : In the base he was to be present.
Rifleman Sanjay Kumar had to return to his camp,
India was at war, in the steep hills that were damp.

Rifleman Sanjay Kumar was a quiet, young man,
who stood at the back of briefings, at the very behind of his clan.
But his work was impeccable, and he was an able soldier,
the launch of the operation was put in a folder.

During the vertical climb, his thoughts drifted away,
to his family back at home. He said, "I must fight for them today!"
And back he was to reality, as enemy shots were fired,
the Indian soldiers, behind a boulder, they retired.

And what followed next, was an astonishing show of skill,
as Rifleman Sanjay Kumar charged ahead for the kill.
He took down an enemy bunker without any help,
grabbing the hot barrel of a gun, entirely by himself.

And towards the enemy he swung it, in the opposite way,
firing it relentlessly, it seemed he had saved the day.
When a barrage of bullets hit him, he collapsed in severe pain,
but he continued fighting with grit, his resilience was maintained.

At the end of the day, the Indians won in a manner of strength,
the price we had to pay was many of our soldiers' death.
But one man was still breathing, and was lying on the ground in pain,
if not for his bravery, India would have had no gain.

Back at Indian home base, a medical team worked hard,
fighting to save his life, they gave him full regards.
And when at last, Rifleman Kumar walked out safe, with a smile,
he returned home a hero, and will remain one for a while.

CAPTAIN VIKRAM BATRA

Year of Award: 1999
Regiment: 13th Battalion, J & K Rifles (JAK RIF)

Captain Vikram Batra

Shershah, he was called, and for good reason, with
indomitable spirit, he always fought treason.
He went down fighting in a noble way,
instrumental in the success of getting Kargil under our sway.

Determined to serve from the time he was born,
his dream came true. The uniform he donned.
He wore it with pride, till the very end,
he saved a comrade, but had to descend.

To get to the top needed a tiring climb,
leading his men, they went on one at a time.
Trembling with fever, he went with his men,
launched an attack, defeated the lion in its den.

During the battle, a bunker he destroyed,
his soldiers and himself were overjoyed.
In the skirmish, his soldier took a hit,
mindless of his safety, he rushed ahead with grit.

He started walking back with his junior on his shoulder,
a bullet hit his back, as they reached the boulder.
Everyone watched in horror, as their commander fell,
his soldiers charged ahead with a tremendous yell!

This brave officer may be gone, but his memory shall be remembered,
he fought with such prowess, his enemies surrendered.
The Param Vir Chakra, he was awarded,
with gallantry and honor, he was lauded!!

GALLERY

Presenting the book and interacting with
General Manoj Pande PVSM, AVSM, VSM, ADC,
Chief of Army Staff, Indian Army

Words of appreciation and presenting the book to
Honorable Defence Minister of India, Shri Rajnath Singh

Presenting the book to Subedar Major Sanjay Kumar PVC and
Subedar Major and Honorary Captain Yogendra Singh Yadav PVC (Retd.),
Param Vir Chakra Winners

Presenting the book to General D.S Suhag PVSM, UYSM, AVSM, VSM, ADC (Retd.), former Chief of Army Staff, Indian Army

With General V.P Malik PVSM, AVSM (Retd.), former Chief of Army Staff, Indian Army

ADG PI · INDIAN ARMY
#MondayMotivation
#IndianArmy salutes 12 year old Master Aditya Kashyap for his tribute to #ParamvirChakra awardees of Indian Armed Forces through his book "India's Heroes – A Tribute". The book is a beautiful compilation of inspiring poems dedicated to the #Paramvirs.
INDIA'S HEROES
A TRIBUTE

Moments...

9 798888 836095